FUN·TO·LEARN

SHAPES

Arianne Holden

Educational Consultant: Dr. Naima Browne

LORENZ BOOKS

NOTES

Fun to Learn Shapes introduces children to the names and properties of different shapes. Each shape is clearly shown and its characteristics are explained. The lively photographs depict familiar objects of the same shape and give suggestions for fun activities.

Reading together
Most children benefit from adult help when reading a book. Do not expect a child to grasp all the information at once! It is better to look at one shape at a time, and then spend a few days letting the information sink in.

Talking it over
Talk about the things you have found out together. Make everyday activities an adventure in learning—look at all the cuboids seen at the supermarket and comment on the shapes of favorite foods such as apples, oranges and so on.

Answering questions
Ask your child questions and encourage him or her to answer. Do not worry if the answers are wrong—making mistakes is part of the learning process. The most important thing is that your child feels confident and willing to try.

Checking your child's understanding
Check that your child understands by asking questions. For example, after you have read about pyramids, find an old travel brochure with a picture of the Egyptian pyramids and see if your child can still recognize the shape.

Learning by doing
Encourage your child to try some of the activities. They have been specially devised to be easy and fun to do. They will also help your child understand that it really is fun to learn!

CONTENTS

Square

This is a square. It has four straight sides, which are exactly the same length, and four matching corners.

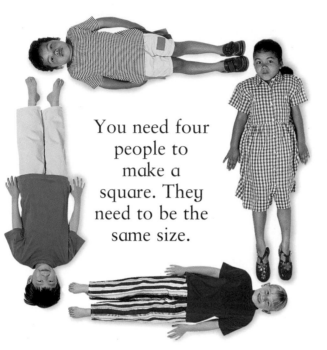

square

You need four people to make a square. They need to be the same size.

Can you count all the squares on my shirt…

…on my pants…

…and on my shoes?

Try this!

Patchwork picture

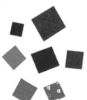

1. Cut out lots of small paper squares from old magazines.

2. Fit the squares together to make a picture.

3. Stick your picture squares onto a piece of paper.

I like painting bright red squares.

Can you find two squares in this picture?

square, blue picture frame

Look at this smiling clown picture in a square frame.

How many squares can you see?

Do you know which games are played on these squares?

Can you see the squares on Teddy's ribbon?

Can you play tic-tac-toe?

What color squares is this teddy wearing?

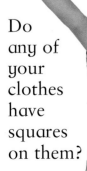
Do any of your clothes have squares on them?

Here is a square envelope...

...for a square card.

Squares fit together without leaving a gap. This is called tessellating.

5

Triangle

A triangle has three straight sides and three corners.

triangles

yummy, chocolate triangles

Sometimes, a triangle has three matching sides and three matching corners.

Three people can make a triangle.

Look at these striped triangles!

What shape is this slice of pizza?

Do you know what this instrument is called?

6

Try this!

Make a string of flags

1. Cut large triangles out of paper.

2. Tape them to a piece of string.

3. Hang the string of flags in your room.

triangular presents

Look at Teddy's triangular hat!

Look at all these triangles. Do any of them have matching sides?

colorful, triangular sails

Can you see any triangles here? How many can you count?

yellow and blue triangular flag

How many triangles are there on this crown?

Triangles will fit together without leaving a space.

7

Circle

A circle is a round shape with no straight sides.

circle

A circle does not have any corners.

A circle will spin…

delicious, circular cookies

How many circles can you see?

...and a circle will roll.

circular wheels on a toy train

Try this!

Make the wheels go round

1. Draw and cut out a car shape on cardboard.

2. Draw and cut out two circles.

3. Draw and cut out two squares.

4. Attach the wheels to the car with paper fasteners. Which wheels turn the best?

Where are the circles on this bike?

You can make patterns with circles.

wobbly, round eyes

You can make circles with...

...your fingers...

...your arms and...

...your mouth!

Rectangle

A rectangle has four straight sides.
It looks like a stretched-out square.

rectangle

A rectangle has...

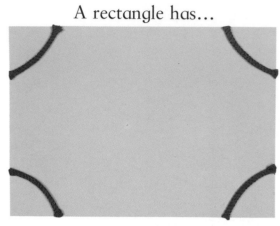

...four matching corners.

How many rectangles can you see here?

What sound will these rectangles make?

rectangles on socks

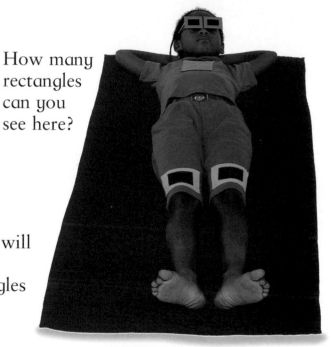

tasty, chocolate rectangles

blue and pink rectangular flag

Do you have a rectangular mirror?

10

a string of rectangular
birthday cards

rectangular, animal dominoes

Try this!

Edible rectangles

1. Ask an
adult to make
you a slice
of toast.

2. Cut the
toast into
fingers.

3. Dip the
rectangular
fingers in
a soft-
boiled
egg—it is
delicious!

Do you use...

...a
rect-
angular
pencil
case...

...a
rectangular
ruler...

...or a
rectangular
calculator
at school?

How many
rectangles
are there
in this
tower?

ZOO

Look at the
rectangular sign.
Where is it pointing?

Rectangles fit together without
leaving a space.

Spiral

A spiral is a smooth, coiled shape without any corners.

spiral

swirly, spiral seashell

spirally skipping rope

tasty, spiral candies

spiral spring...

...BOING!

slithery, spirally snails

Follow the spiral shoelace trail.

Can you see the spirals in the pen?

You can drink through this spiral.

spiral china cat

spirally hair

Teddy's T-shirt has a pink spiral on it!

Try this!

Make a spiral pot

1. Roll some clay into a long, thin sausage shape.

2. Curl your clay around in a spiral.

3. Build up the sides by winding the clay around.

Look at the spiral on the spinning top!

Can you paint a spiral?

What is this spiral made from?

You can make patterns with spirals.

Diamond

A diamond has four matching, straight sides. How is it different from a square?

diamond

diamond trellis

delightful, diamond kites

diamond playing cards

Look at all the diamonds on my suit!

Did you know?

You can make a diamond out of two triangles.

colorful, diamond drum

Diamonds fit together without leaving a space.

14

Semicircle

A semicircle is half a circle.
It has one curved side and
one straight side.

semicircle

You can make a semicircle!

Sometimes,
the sun
looks
like a
semicircle.

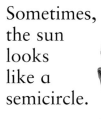

What is
Teddy
juggling?

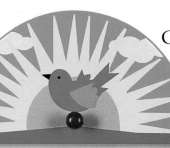

What is this
semicircle
called?

Can you see the
bird on this
semicircular
hook?

Can you paint
a sunrise?

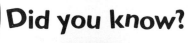

Did you know?

You can make a
circle out of two
semicircles.

Semicircles will fit
together, but the
circles leave gaps.

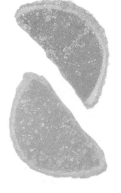

15

Heart

A heart is a curved shape with a dip in the top. Hearts make people think of love.

shiny, heart balloons

heart

Teddies LO♥E hearts

Try this!

Make a love heart

1. Fold a big piece of red paper in half. Draw half a heart on it.

2. Cut it out, then open it up, and you have a heart.

3. Draw all the things you love.

4. Stick them on your love heart.

To whom would you give this cake?

heart-shaped chocolates

Can you see the heart I am wearing?

Hearts will fit together, but they leave spaces in between.

Star

A star has several straight sides that join together to make points.

crisp, yellow starfruit

star

glittery, golden star

What do you think the frog will turn into?

Did you know?

You can make a star out of two triangles.

funny, starry sunglasses

star-shaped candles

Stars fit together, but they leave spaces in between.

Cube

A cube is a solid shape with six matching, square sides.

cube

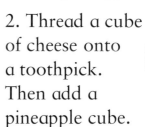

tumbling cube dice

Do you think there is anything inside the three pretty cube boxes?

Try this!

Cubes on sticks

1. Cut some cheese and pineapple cubes.

2. Thread a cube of cheese onto a toothpick. Then add a pineapple cube.

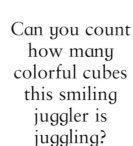

Can you count how many colorful cubes this smiling juggler is juggling?

3. Thread on one more cheese cube for a tasty treat!

colorful building blocks

Sometimes, candles are cubes. What other shapes can you see on the candle?

What shape is this crane hoisting up?

Do you like giving presents?

crunchy, brown sugar cubes

Teddy is building a tower of cubes.

What shape is this present?

What is inside the box?

Peekaboo!

19

Cuboid

A cuboid is a solid shape with six flat sides.

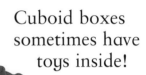

cuboid

big, blue, cuboid truck

Cuboid boxes sometimes have toys inside!

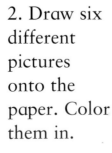

Try this!

Cuboid picture box

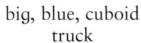

1. Ask an adult to copy the shape of a cuboid box onto paper.

2. Draw six different pictures onto the paper. Color them in.

3. Glue the pictures onto the box.

What shape is the ice in this glass?

cold, chocolate ice-cream cuboid

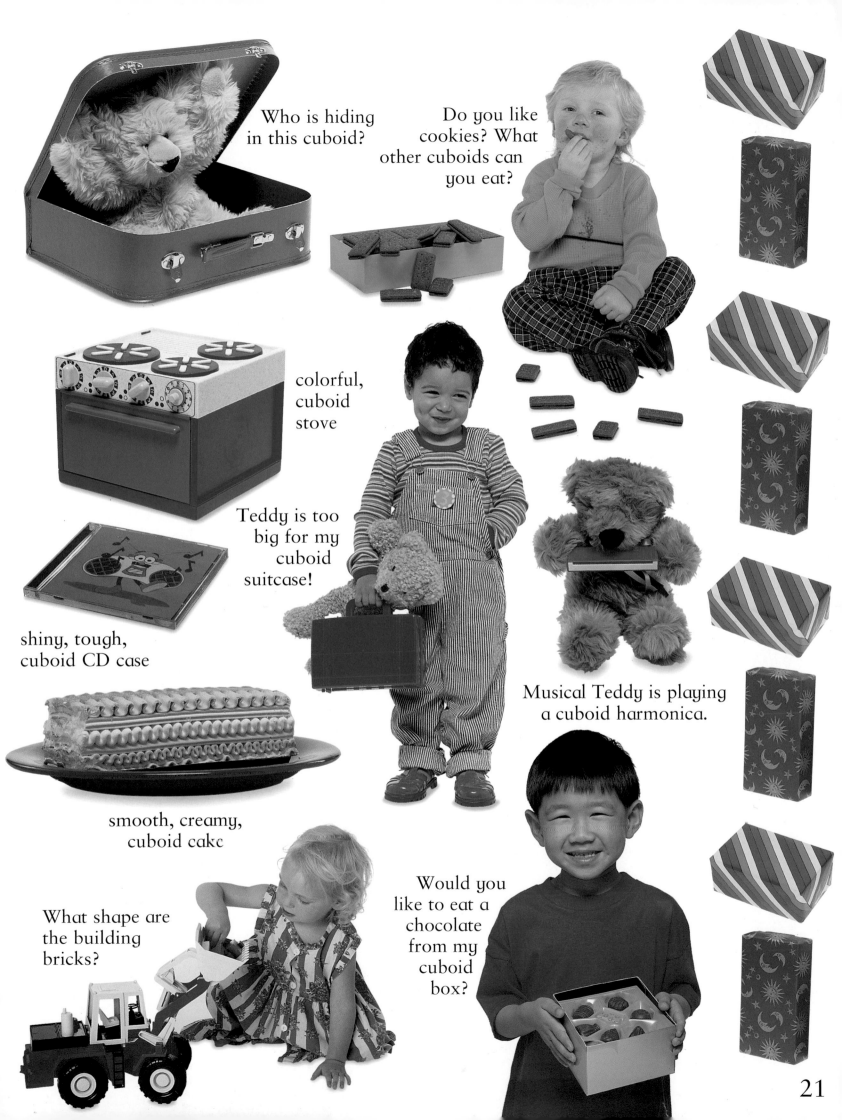

Who is hiding in this cuboid?

Do you like cookies? What other cuboids can you eat?

colorful, cuboid stove

Teddy is too big for my cuboid suitcase!

shiny, tough, cuboid CD case

Musical Teddy is playing a cuboid harmonica.

smooth, creamy, cuboid cake

What shape are the building bricks?

Would you like to eat a chocolate from my cuboid box?

21

Cylinder

A cylinder is a solid shape.
It has a circle at each end
and one smooth curved face.

cylinder

These cylinders have…

…cylindrical beads inside them!

Tins can be cylinders.

a tall tower of cylinders

How many cylinders can you see here?

You can play with cylinders!

What would you do with these cylinders?

You can save money in this cylinder!

cylindrical rolls of
wrapping paper

cylinders
full of
sparkly
glitter

What
shape is the
telescope?

Sometimes, you can crawl through cylinders.

Try this!

Cylinder stamps

1. Ask an adult for the cork from a wine bottle.

2. Paint a face on one end.

3. Stamp the cork on a piece of paper.

What sound does this cylinder make?

noisy, tooting cylinders

Pyramid

A pyramid is a solid shape, with four triangular faces.

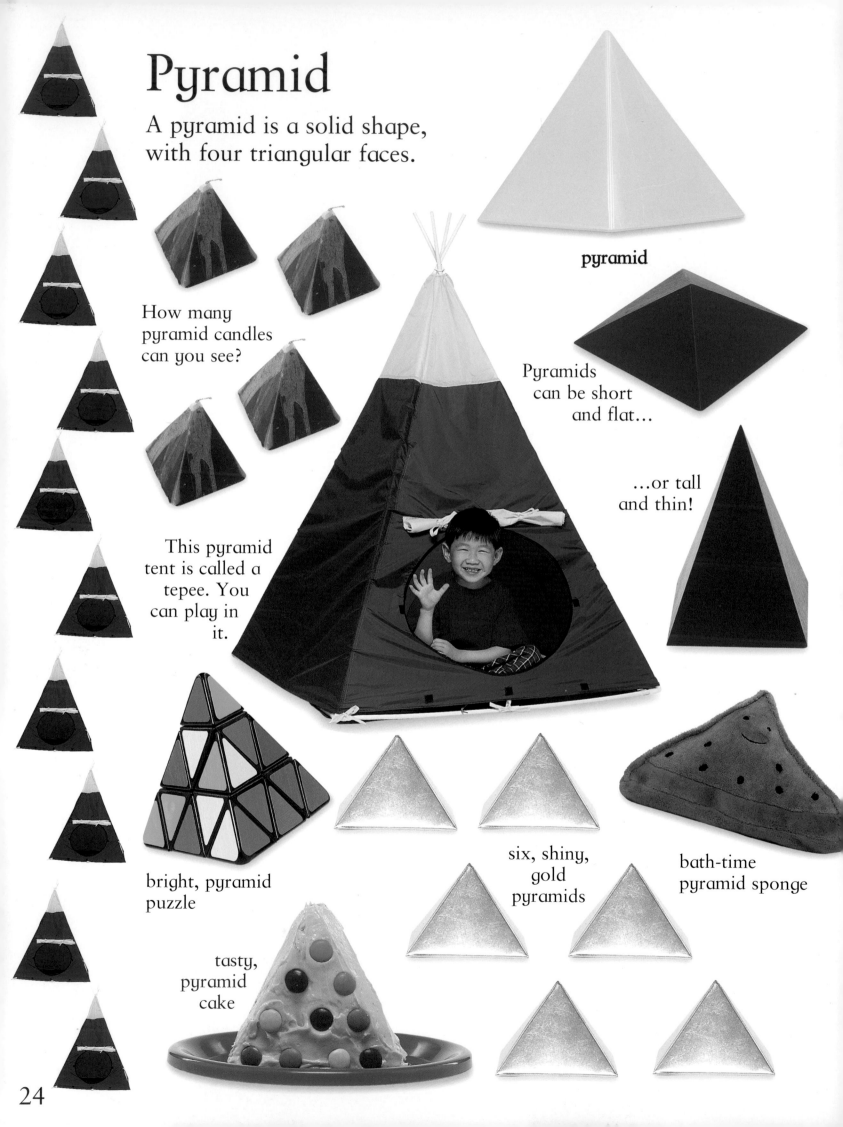

pyramid

How many pyramid candles can you see?

Pyramids can be short and flat...

...or tall and thin!

This pyramid tent is called a tepee. You can play in it.

bright, pyramid puzzle

six, shiny, gold pyramids

bath-time pyramid sponge

tasty, pyramid cake

Cone

A cone is a solid shape with a pointed end, and one curved face.

cone

funny party hats

5

What's inside this cone?

Cones are perfect for holding ice cream…

Peekaboo!

….or candy!

Coneheads

1. Draw a big circle on a big piece of thin cardboard.

2. Cut it out. Bend in from the edge to the middle.

3. Slide one edge under the other to make a cone. When it fits on your head, stick it together with glue.

happy clown in a cone hat

A big cone like this can make your voice sound LOUDER.

Sphere

A sphere is a round solid shape, with no edges or corners.

sphere

Look at this enormous sphere. Would you like to play with it?

What shape are the bubbles?

Can you balance a sphere on your head?

These spheres have funny faces.

Pom-poms are spheres.

Look at our hair elastics!

What shape is this pumpkin?

Look at me! I'm bobbing for apples.

crisp, spherical apples

Try this!

Make a spherical necklace

1. Roll some clay into spheres. Make a hole in the middle of them.

2. Thread your spheres onto a piece of cord. Now you can wear your spheres.

juicy, spherical oranges

Quick, Jake! Catch the ball before it rolls away.

Spheres are great for juggling! Can you juggle?

Shapes in nature

Shapes are everywhere. Look around you and see what shapes you can see.

Can you see the heart shape on the snake's skin?

What shape are these tomatoes?

When you cut a watermelon in half you can see a circle.

shiny, red, spherical berries

round, shiny apples

What shape are the kitten's ears?

Ferns have tightly curled spiral leaves.

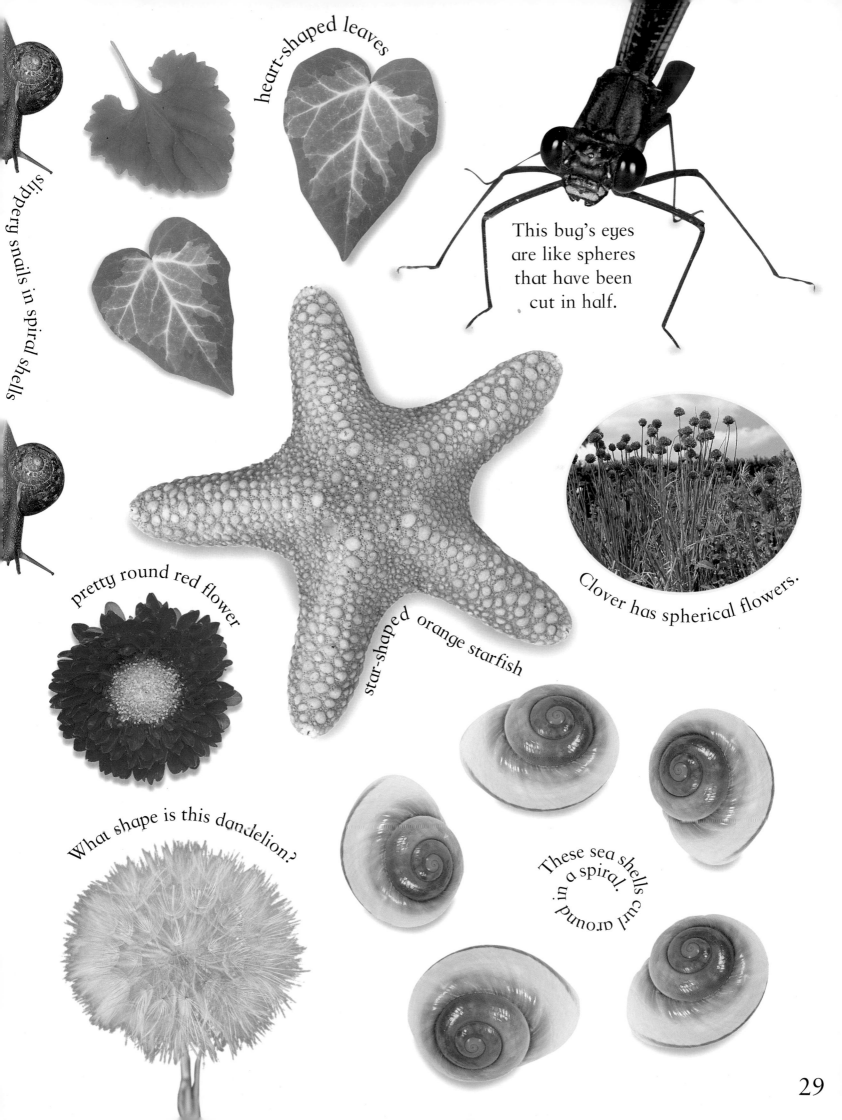

slippery snails in spiral shells

heart-shaped leaves

This bug's eyes are like spheres that have been cut in half.

Clover has spherical flowers.

pretty round red flower

star-shaped orange starfish

What shape is this dandelion?

These sea shells curl around in a spiral.

29

Shapes race

The snails, Wiggly William and Curly Kate, are going to see the semicircle juggler. Roll a die and move your marker to see who will get there first.

markers or buttons

die

Wiggly William

Curly Kate

START

1

2

3

4 Pass the Square Bears. Move onto the next yellow square.

5

6

7 Stop to listen to Triangle Ted. Miss a turn.

8

9

10 Meet the Heart Bears. Move onto the next heart.

11

15

16

17

The Diamond Clown is very lucky. Take another turn.

14

13

12

18

19

20

Find a cube present. Go forward 2 spaces.

21

22

23

24

25

You have reached the semicircle juggler. How many semicircles can you see?

FINISH

First published in 1998 by Lorenz Books
27 West 20th Street, New York, NY 10011

LORENZ BOOKS are available for bulk purchase for sales promotion and for
premium use. For details, write or call the sales director, Lorenz Books,
27 West 20th Street, New York, NY 10011;
(800) 354-9657

ISBN 1 85967 682 0

Publisher: Joanna Lorenz
Managing Editor, Children's Books: Sue Grabham
Project Manager: Belinda Weber
Consultant: Dr. Naima Browne, Department of Education, University of London
Design and Typesetting: Val Carless
Photography: John Freeman
Head Stylist: Marion Elliott
Stylists: Ken Campbell, Melanie Williams

The Publishers would like to thank the following children for modeling in this book:
Rosie Anness, Harriet Bartholomew, Jonathan Bartholomew, Daisy Bartlett, Chilli
Bernstein, Andrew Brown, April Cain, Freddy Cassford, Milo Clare, Matthew
Ferguson, Patriche Frith, Troy Frith, Saffron George, Madison Harrington, Faye
Harrison, Becky Johnson, Holly Matthews, Jack Matthews, Rebekah Murrell, Philip
Quach, Eloise Shepherd

Picture credits: 28 BR Zefa; 29 CR © W Broadhurst, FLPA, BL © Zefa-Oster

Printed in Hong Kong / China

1 3 5 7 9 10 8 6 4 2